ULSTER IN THE VIKING AGE

A View to a Conquest

Michael Sheane

ARTHUR H. STOCKWELL LTD
Torrs Park   Ilfracombe   Devon
Established 1898
www.ahstockwell.co.uk

British Library Cataloguing-in-Publication Data.
A catalogue record for this book is available
from the British Library.

By the same author:
Ulster & Its Future After the Troubles (1977)
Ulster & The German Solution (1978)
Ulster & The British Connection (1979)
Ulster & The Lords of the North (1980)
Ulster & The Middle Ages (1982)
Ulster & St Patrick (1984)
The Twilight Pagans (1990)
Enemy of England (1991)
The Great Siege (2002)
Ulster in the Age of Saint Comgall of Bangor (2004)
Ulster Blood (2005)
King William's Victory (2006)
Ulster Stock (2007)
Famine in the Land of Ulster (2008)
Pre-Christian Ulster (2009)
The Glens of Antrim (2010)
Ulster Women (2010)
Tne Invasion of Ulster (2010)

ISBN 978-0-7223-4085-1
Printed in Great Britain by
Arthur H. Stockwell Ltd
Torrs Park   Ilfracombe
Devon

Contents

Chapter 1

The Viking Menace

Some historians believe that the Vikings reached Ireland as early as the fourth century. They were farmers as well as conquerors. This was the age of the decline of the Roman Empire in the east and these Viking raiders reached as far away as present-day Istanbul and Russia, led by the fierce Rurik, a Viking sea king.

The date AD 795 seems a more likely date for the coming of the Norsemen (Norwegians, Swedes and Danes). It appears that the Danes were last upon the scene. These Vikings were a violent race, despite evidence that they farmed the land in Ulster and the rest of Ireland. At the end of the eighth century, the Norse were sighted off Rathlin Island in present-day County Antrim, and here they put the monks and other inhabitants to death, erecting statues of Thor and overthrowing Christ. The Vikings were fiercely pagan and mocked the Marian Church. No matter how much the people prayed, the Vikings continued their onslaught. At Rathlin the dragon-headed longships came out of the mist as the oars fell and rose in rhythm. Those standing at the prow of the ships were young men. Many of them had blond hair and cold blue eyes that glittered with excitement.

The word 'Viking' meant to make war by sea. The longships could travel anywhere where there was enough water. Norway and Sweden had a much indented coastline, and here in the fjords the Vikings practised their warlike arts. The climate is unsuited to farming, for the summers are short and the winters are long. Many crops will not grow in the land, and it is too rocky to plough. The Vikings were thus dependent upon the sea to support their families. Life was perilous.

From earliest times the Vikings had built boats. At first they used dugout canoes, rather like early Irish curraghs. They were made by hollowing out a single tree trunk. They also made hide-covered vessels, using skins stretched over wooden frames and lashed together with leather thongs. These were simple fishing boats and they were only able to sail small distances, unlike the longships of a later date. By the eighth century, they had learned to build longships, so they could launch attacks upon other lands in Western Europe, and explore the seas. In Ulster they built settlements on the shores of Lough Foyle, Larne Lough, Strangford Lough and Carlingford Lough.

The Vikings discovered that people in distant lands traded extensively, exchanging goods and produce for whatever they required. Some of these items were luxury goods which the Norse did not have, and they wanted to take part in trade also. The Vikings, however, at first were not wealthy. They were hardly able to feed and clothe themselves, and they did not have much surplus for the purpose of trade. However, their ships were soon sailing along the great trade routes, and they began to compete with other peoples.

It was not long before the Norsemen started to plunder their neighbours. Sometimes their meagre supplies would run out, so they leaped ashore to kill and loot. Before long they realized that sea-raiding could provide them with an important source of wealth. The raids may have started almost by accident, when Vikings in boats ran out of supplies. Attack and conquest became a way of life, as the Vikings stole what they needed from coastal settlements all around the North Sea. They were not peaceful traders, but wild and reckless men. With increasing success, they became bolder and bolder. All around the coast of Ireland, they slew the menfolk, stole their valuables and captured women and children to sell into slavery.

The success of the Norwegians prompted the Danes to adopt similar tactics, and other raiders came from the Orkney Islands and the Hebrides. They all came under the heading of what modern history records as the Norsemen. The Irish, and others that feared them, called them Vikings. In AD 795, when the Vikings approached the coast of Ireland, perhaps for the first time, much of Ulster was covered in forests, and when they arrived back home they spoke about the green island of Erin where great trees grew, for timber was essential for building their longships.

It has been recorded that the Norsemen made a second visit to the north of Ireland in AD 797. As they passed the Skerries, off the north coast of County Dublin, they could make out stone churches and clusters of monastic buildings. The buildings were Christian monasteries on one of the islands, known as Lambay.

The Vikings must have been weary with the rowing, but the longships sped forward as though without effort. The prow of each longship was deeply carved and painted to look like a great dragon rising out of the waves. The sight struck terror into the Gaels. The Vikings were building a great trading empire, which already stretched as far east as Russia. The largest of the longships could carry more than 120 warriors and had thirty-four pairs of oars as well as the large square sail.

Many Vikings were peaceful traders, but those that went conquering were most adored at home. They brought back thrilling stories about the Gaels and other faraway peoples.

Most lads dreamed of becoming Viking warriors, for they considered them to be heroes. Some of the girls may have dreamed of becoming Vikings also, but the women did not usually go on long sea voyages. When the warriors were away they did all the work. They were skilled in ploughing and herding, and they could sail a small fishing vessel as well as a man could.

Norwegian houses were built of timber. They were robust, and usually rectangular with steeply pitched roofs. Some had turf on the roofs to insulate them from the snow. The Vikings ate oxen, pigs, goats and deer, and raised geese for both meat and eggs. Fish and whale meat also formed a large part of their diet.

Viking warriors wore long, snug-fitting woollen trousers and short tunics. They sported leather boots, which were bound around their lower legs with thongs. They also wore bearskin cloaks, pinned at the shoulder, which left their arms free for combat. Their heads were protected by conical helmets with a nosepiece and ear flaps. It is commonly thought that the Vikings wore horned helmets into battle; but if that were so, an enemy could grab a warrior by the horns and twist his neck enough to break it.

The strongest warriors carried a triangular battleaxe, which was so heavy that it took two hands to wield it. Other men had swords and spears.

The Vikings believed that a warrior who died in combat went straight to Valhalla, the Vikings' heaven. The bards in the warriors' homeland sang songs about him after his death.

The first Gaelic monks to meet the Vikings welcomed their visitors and invited them to share in their humble meal, for Christian hospitality was part of their daily routine. A typical meal might have consisted of coarse brown bread, dried fruit and boiled vegetables. The monks, perhaps at Rathlin, showed the Vikings around their island. They probably made no effort

8

to conceal the gold chalices on the altar of their chapel or their precious illuminated manuscripts of the Gospels. The monks at Rathlin were probably eager to show these symbols of their faith to the Vikings. The monks hoped for converts.

What the monks received from the Vikings was the threat of death, and they lost everything of value. The Vikings set fire to the buildings on Rathlin and other islands and took to the sea. The surviving monks thanked God for life. They prayed that the Viking raiders would not come back.

The Vikings returned to their snow-covered homeland to tell their adventures to the womenfolk and to show their booty to jealous neighbours. Before long, a new expedition was ready to sail to the north of Ireland. The expedition left amid scenes of great excitement. The women, left behind, sang as they baked bread; they wore clothes made from cloth and dyed wool; they tended milch cows and ploughed the rocky fields in the absence of their menfolk. The women lived in hope of the gold and silver that the warriors would bring back. Children played at plundering, staging mock battles, which the Vikings always won. When the time came for the warriors' return, the women would keep a lookout. The tension mounted until, at last, the square sails of the longships were sighted in the fjords.

Chapter 2

Viking Intentions

Eighth-century Ulster was, like the rest of Ireland, a prosperous place. It had rich grasslands that supported cattle, as well as dense forests of oak, yew and fir trees. The forests were alive with game, whilst the lakes and rivers teemed with fish. There was gold to be found in the rivers and streams. The climate in Ulster was quite mild compared to that of the Norse countries. Ireland had not been invaded in historic times, and even the Roman conquest of Europe did not include the island. However, this did not mean that Ulster was a peaceful land. As in the rest of Ireland, there were a number of different tribes, with as many as 250 tribal kings or *rís*. The *rís* paid tribute to the kings of the provinces of Munster, Leinster, Ulster and Connaught. These provincial kings also paid taxes to the High King, who ruled from Tara in the 'fifth' province, Meath. Each tribal king had his own army, which would fight for no one else. These kings did not unite into a 'national' state. For many centuries the Gaels lived in some kind of unity, for the High King would travel his kingdoms, but in many places he was despised. The High King had his own army to protect him. He was like a king of kings.

The Gaels were descended from warrior aristocracy. Like

the Vikings, they enjoyed fighting. They fought for cattle and for glory.

With the coming of the Church, reading and writing brought literacy to the island, which many claim was evangalized by St Patrick. Monastery schools such as the one at Clonmacnoise were well-known throughout Europe. Monastic sites like Armagh, Derry and, of course, Downpatrick, were the nearest thing Ulster had to cities. Outside these monasteries the Gaels lived by cattle-farming and hunting. Ireland was rich in natural resources, so they had no need to farm the sea. A few Irish tribes mined gold in the Antrim Hills, and here at Slieve Mish, St Patrick tended sheep owned by Miliuc, the local king.

Viking raids became increasingly frequent.

The island of Iona, off the east coast of Scotland, was the site of a famous monastery. It is likely that the famous Book of Kells, a lovely illuminated manuscript, was written here. A scribe working on similar books in the scriptorium would have used small sheets of gold leaf for decorating and illuminating the pages. The monks who created these holy objects kept supplies of gold and silver and gemstones. The monks' workshops were peaceful places, with sunlight beaming through a long row of windows under the eaves. Here chalices and candlesticks were engraved. The monks emphasized the holiness of their art, and in the background as they worked monks continued to chant. In otherwise virtual silence, the monks occupied themselves with work and prayer.

The Vikings did not respect the religious significance of the holy objects. They had no use for the illuminated books, but they coveted the shrines which had contained them. These were made of precious metals that could be melted down and gemstones that could be prised off. They also took the gold chalices and plates and anything else of value they could lay their hands on.

In AD 806 a party of Norsemen killed sixty-eight monks on

11

Iona. Some of the terrified survivors fled to Ireland bringing news of the cruel Vikings and their hatred of Christ.

After the raid, the Vikings sailed homeward with a ship full of sparkling plunder. Their women were overjoyed. This plunder, so easily taken, would raise the quality of their lives. The Norse traders found that they could obtain high prices for the plunder on the European mainland, for Gaelic craftsmanship was highly valued. Irish gold could be exchanged in the Mediterranean for wine, silk and spices.

Irish scholars found themselves recording one Viking raid after another as more and more longships appeared off the coast of Ulster – indeed, of Ireland in general. They swooped in from the sea and carried out bloody raids, and the Gaels could not defend themselves. The Norsemen made no attempt to probe inland, away from coastal areas. It was perhaps some time before the Norsemen rowed up the River Bann in the north of the island, or the broad River Shannon after rowing down the Atlantic coast.

The history of these years is fragmentary, for the Norsemen burned the annals and histories. Everywhere they set up statues to Odin and Thor.

Fjords like Larne Lough (Ulfrek's Fjord) were alive with Viking ships, and here battles must have taken place between different groups of the invaders themselves. Little settlements like Laharna were obliterated in the early years of the Viking invasions of Ulster. Inland from Larne, dark forests were inhabited by hostile Irish tribes, and places like Slemish, in mid-Antrim, lay untouched by the invaders in the ninth century. At Antrim town, however, there is an impressive round tower that must have been erected in the later period of Viking invasions. From the top of towers like this, of which there are many in Ulster, the defenders pelted the Norsemen with stones.

If danger threatened the Vikings, they could always retreat to their longships.

Monks were not trained fighting men, but the Norsemen were violent as a matter of course. Conquest was to whet the appetite for more blood and booty. As the raids increased so also did the building of round towers. These also provided lookout positions for the monks. They would see the ships before they landed and hear the cries of the Norsemen as they went through the fields and climbed the rising ground around the Antrim Hills and the Mourne Mountains. The round towers were also used to house valuables, including the sacred vessels of the church. The only door of the tower was above ground level and was reached by a wooden ladder. Once the monks sighted the Vikings, they climbed into the tower and pulled up the ladder after them, so all the Vikings could do was to shout at the monks.

They invoked the Norse god of war, Thor, and they carried statues of the god with them. These statues were coloured. The Norsemen bowed down before their pagan images. Very few things discouraged the Vikings. They were a brawny, fair-haired people.

Any study of the Viking Age in Ulster requires reference to the extant annals, in which sea sagas are sometimes recorded. Raids are recorded as having taken place over many decades. However, the records do not record everything chronologically, and references to some raids aren't duplicated. In some accounts of raids on churches, church events are mentioned. The most serious raids seem to have taken place between AD 821 and 850. In the Annals, forty-four ninth-century raids are recorded, and another source tells of a cluster of fifteen raids between 881 and 890. A full treatment of the Viking raids up to the eleventh century is available in the various Annals of Ireland and of Ulster. There seems to have been a concentration of raiding between 820 and 840. However, the Annals record a dramatic declined in raids after 830.

It is not easy to draw conclusions about the Vikings in the history of the island; basically the Vikings invaded both parts of Ireland equally. The proximity to the mainland of counties Antrim and Down meant they received the brunt of the raids, with York (Jorvik) in the north-east of England as the Viking centre of operations to invade and conquer Ireland.

The distance between Rathlin Island and Scotland is about twelve miles, and on a clear day even small boats off the Scottish coast can be seen from Torr Head in North Antrim.

The Annals are not homogeneous in style, being the work of a number of writers. Most of these writers were churchmen.

The Viking grip lasted well into the eleventh century, when the Norsemen were defeated at the Battle of Clontarf.

Christianity seems to have gone into a steep decline after the 830s, but the Church looked back to the example of St Patrick, St Columba and St Comgall, so that the Gaels would hold on to their faith in the truth of Christianity.

From the ninth century, Vikings were active all around the coast of the British Isles, but particularly in the North Channel and Irish Sea.

The monastery of Whithorn in Galloway was destroyed by fire in 830. It was occupied later in the ninth century by a community with Norse connections. By the eleventh century it was a busy trading post. It boasted square-timbered houses.

By the eighth-century, Ireland was quite a centre for art, literature and learning. Despite the lack of a central kingship, the Gaelic elite of Ulster developed some kind of Irish identity based on language, culture and religion.

The incoming Vikings were divided into light-haired and dark-haired foreigners. The Vikings have been credited with the establishment of towns in Ireland, chiefly along the Irish coast. In Ulster, Larne (or Laharna) springs to mind.

There is a school of thought that the Norsemen did not arrive directly from Scandinavia. They adopted aspects of Gaelic culture, so it is perhaps useful to describe them as Hiberno-Norse.

The Vikings were not the only ones raiding Irish monasteries, for raiding was endemic in early Christian Ulster. There are thirty recorded attacks by the Gaels prior to the Vikings' arrival at Rathlin Island.

Up to the early tenth century, there is a clear distinction between the Norsemen and the Gaels. After this the differences become blurred. Raids in the north and south of Ireland followed the same pattern as in England. From the 830s isolated coastal attacks on monasteries gave way to inland expeditions. The Vikings now had larger fleets, and they constructed fortified camps known as longphorts.

The inland raids led to the establishment of Armagh as an important centre, for here was the ancient capital of Ulster. Armagh lay about fifty miles from the coast at the North Channel and Irish Sea. It is thought that the Vikings rowed up the River Bann from the Coleraine region, to occupy lands around Lough Neagh. Lough Neagh is the largest lake in the British Isles, and it dominates the map of Ulster. It may have taken the Norsemen two or three hours to reach the lake, along the calmer waters of the river (as opposed to the rough seas of the North Channel and around the Scottish isles).

The Gaels, lining the shores of the river, watched the Norsemen row up the Bann. They were sure that the Vikings would launch an attack upon them. The monks prayed to Christ and the Virgin Mary that they would be preserved from Viking horrors.

The Pope in Rome prayed for the welfare of the Gaels, as he did for the victims of the Norsemen throughout Europe. These raiders were now at the peak of their fighting prowess, and the Gaels recorded them, perhaps with exaggeration, as being formidable enemies.

The Christians were aware that the Norsemen would set up an altar to Thor in the Catholic cathedral at Armagh. Here the fierce sea king Turgesius set up a statue. The Vikings prayed to their gods, and particularly to Thor.

This was the situation that obtained from 795 to 1054, but the worst of the attacks were over, it is thought, by the tenth century. Pressures of population may have driven the Norsemen from their homelands to conquer and occupy lands like Ulster. The Vikings set up important bases at Armagh and Dublin.

Chapter 3

How the Ulstermen Lived

Life in an Irish monastery followed strict rules, for the monks rose before dawn and spent their days in work and prayer. The monks kept livestock and grew their own crops. They often brewed beer and made mead (a thick, sweet wine made from apples and honey). The word 'honeymoon' comes from the custom whereby couples drank only mead for the first month after marriage. The monks did not drink mead; they traded it for other items that they needed. Their diet was very plain. They lived on coarse bread, porridge, vegetables and beer. Dried fruit was only eaten on important feast days.

The monasteries were not only centres of religious life, for they also provided education for the children of the nobility. Nobility from distant lands sent their offspring to Ireland's great schools, at places such as Derry and Armagh in the north. Throughout the Christian era the remote islands off the coast were known as a repository of learning.

The monasteries of Ireland did not enjoy peace even before the coming of the Vikings. In both the north and the south, kings and their warriors sometimes sacked and looted the monasteries. The treasures of the monks were not free from the clutches of the greedy kings.

Life outside these communities was a very different matter. The land was rich in game, so the Gaels ate a lot of meat. Wild boar was a favourite. The thighs of the wild boar were called the 'champions portion', and they were set aside for the heroes of the tribes – the best warriors. In Gaelic mythology, the hero Cúchulainn was always given the champions portion. The brains and the liver were reserved for chieftains and bards.

Hunters provided their families with deer meat; some beef and mutton may also have been eaten. Cattle were kept mainly to provide leather and milk, while sheep were prized for their wool.

Many varieties of fish, including shellfish, were eaten. Eels were boiled in milk. Some Gaels liked badger meat, which is quite fatty.

Every household made its own butter, and buttermilk was a favourite drink, but there were no potatoes in ancient Ireland, the potato having come from America. The Gaels ate barley and other grains, and pulses, they grew onions and root vegetables, harvested with garlic and mushrooms. Honey was a favourite food, and there were special laws governing the keeping of bees.

Homesteads in the north of Ireland, as in the south, were protected by circular banks and ditches. The houses within these earthworks were mainly built of timber or a type of wickerwork called 'wattle and daub'. The roundhouses were thatched with rushes and had a fireplace with a stone kerb. The outside was covered with limewash, either left white or highly coloured with natural pigments. The larger dwellings of the nobility were sometimes divided into separate 'rooms' by timber screens, which could be moved about. These buildings often stood on raised mounds.

Well-to-do families covered their beds with woven sheets and embroidered coverlets. They dined on low tables, using knives but no forks. They drank from cups, goblets and drinking horns. Sometimes they used napkins, and almost every household had basins for bathing. It was the custom to offer guests warm water as soon as they arrived.

There were numerous laws in ancient Ireland. The people obeyed a system known as the Brehon Law, which was administered by judges called brehons. The kings had absolute authority over their fellows. It is thought that there were no police or prisons, but each tribe was responsible for its own members. If a Gael broke the law, he was declared an outlaw. This meant he was outside the law, and the law would no longer protect him. An outlaw lived in disgrace all his life. No one wanted to know him, and his children had no rights of inheritance. He might be killed for his garments or for the food in his bowl. If the law demanded compensation, and the transgressor was unable to pay it, his entire tribe had to pay it for him. Therefore a tribe, or *tuath*, made every effort to ensure that its members did not break the law.

Cattle-raiding was not regarded as a crime; it was almost like sport in ancient Ulster. Ulstermen went on cattle raids in the same way as the Norsemen went plundering. Since the Gaels had no money, wealth was determined by the number of cattle a man had. A Gael that owned many cattle was called a *bóaire*, or cattle lord.

Tribes were made up of several clans and all the members of the tribe were related to one another by blood or marriage. Normally the chieftain of the strongest clan became king of the tribe. The king and his warriors protected the tribe and defended its land. The king did not own the tribal lands, but he was responsible for them.

Kings and chieftains were the only people to possess horses. These were small animals in comparison with horses today, and they were used for riding, or to pull a chariot. At one stage warriors used chariots in battle, but by the time the Vikings reached Ulster chariots were merely used ceremonially. The

Irish used leather saddles, but not stirrups. The saddles were sometimes made of beautifully decorated leather and the saddlecloths were often embroidered.

Ordinary folk walked wherever they pleased. To reach summer pasturage, entire families would walk for miles on foot, driving their cattle before them. The family would pass the season with their herds, sheltering in huts. Most cattle raids took place during the summer, as did fights between clans and tribes.

Gaelic warfare was often strictly formalized. Sometimes battles were fought between single champions, and both sides accepted the result. This prevented too many men from being killed in an island that did not have a large population. After a battle, the survivors on both sides sometimes feasted together and celebrated one another's bravery.

In winter the rain and mud made fighting difficult, so the people stayed at home. By the light of candles they repaired their tools and weapons and told stories around the fires. Storytelling was their principal form of entertainment. The Gaels also loved music, and they had a variety of instruments, such as harps, pipes and drums.

Because the Gaels of Ulster had enough to eat and were well used to raiding amongst themselves, they at first did not realize the immense threat of the Norsemen. The attacks on the monasteries did not have much effect on the ordinary Ulsterman. The raids of course ceased when the Vikings returned to their homelands for the winter.

The more the Norsemen saw of Ulster, the more they liked it. Their presence would have an effect upon everyone. Storm clouds were gathering in Ulster, and they would soon sweep the entire island.

As the centuries elapsed the round towers were used as quarries to provide stone for building churches. The towers varied in size, some reaching 200 feet in height and over eighty feet in diameter at the base. The entrance was twenty feet or so above the ground. The towers were divided into storeys about ten feet high, each having four lancet openings to the cardinal points of the compass. The roof was conical, made up of overlapping stone slabs, and a circle of carved heads and other ornamentation could sometimes be found beneath the projecting cornice. The masonry was of hewn stone, and blocks of every size and shape can be found in a single tower.

The surviving towers occupy situations close to existing churches, abbeys or other church buildings. This has led many historians to believe that the towers were definitely built by the monks. It is reasonable to assume, therefore, that the monks' valuables were stored in these structures during the Viking raids.

The towers do not seem to have been intended as belfries, as in nearly every case the neighbouring church has a bell tower of its own. They were not built as hermit cells, as is apparent from the fact that hermit caves and cells are common not only in Ulster but in the rest of Ireland and are generally in secluded spots. However, from time to time some of the round towers were adapted to each of these uses.

There is some evidence that the round towers were not built by the monks at all. The monastic writers were fond of recording what they built and how they went about it, but nowhere do they record the building of a round tower.

The round towers are almost certainly pagan in origin, predating written history. There is little doubt that the early Gaelic pagans were sun- and fire-worshippers, and the round towers were built by the Druids for the purposes of worship. Dawn is of primary importance to sun-worshippers, and all the towers have extensive views to the east, where the sun rises. Deposits of ashes and embers at the base of the towers are consistent with the idea that a sacred fire was kept burning.

The Gaelic name for a round tower is a *colcagh* ('fire god'), and the Gaelic word for fire is often in the names of the towers, or the hills, mountains or islands where they are situated.

Most of the towers are near springs or wells, still regarded as holy. Miraculous tales are told about some of the towers. There are legends of sacred towers, some being associated with a local saint or hero.

Towers of similar structure are to be found throughout Europe. In mountainous and hilly districts of Brittany, there are several towers almost identical to those of Ireland. There are others in Sardinia. In Minorca there is the famous Tower of Alaoir. The mountainous and hilly regions of Southern Italy also have round towers. Malta has the Goianby's Tower. In many ways these are identical to the Tower of Cashel in Ireland.

There is some evidence that the round towers of Ireland were erected by a people with a similar religion to the natives of India. In India, local traditions tell how their towers were built miraculously in a single night, and similar legends exist in Ireland. In the early morning's light a tower rose towards the sky on the spot where, the evening before, no preparation for building had been visible.

It is said that the Tower of Tullaherin was built in one night by a monk who came to the district as a missionary. He found the locals inhospitable, and he was unable to obtain lodgings for the night. He decided to remain, believing that a place more in need of missionary work could not be found in Ireland. On the evening of his arrival, he began to build, and by morning the tower was built. He took up his bed in it, preaching at the entrance to the crowds attracted by rumours of his miracles.

The story of the Tower of Aghagower is similar, save in one particular: the saint in this case was helped by an angel.

Kilmacduagh was built in one night, it is said, by angels without human assistance, while a saint watched and prayed.

Ballygaddy has a legend no less spectacular: a giant of the neighbourhood, having received a hostile message from another giant, took a stand at Ballygaddy Hill so that he could watch for his adversary. For seven days and nights he stood upon the hill, and at the end of this time his legs were so tired that he thought they might give way under him. He built the tower as a support for his tired body. The giant who proposed the encounter finally faced him in battle and there was not a whole bone left in the blackguard's ugly carcass. After the battle the victor started to kick arrogantly at the tower.

The Tower of Ardpatrick was, according to tradition, built under the direction of one of Ireland's great saints, while the high tower on the Rock of Cashel is attributed by the same authority to Cormac Macarthy, king archbishop of Cashel. He was engaged in a dispute with a neighbour and he needed a watchtower, so he summoned all his people to build it in one night. At sunrise he was able to ascertain the location of the opposing army; and at sunrise he gave it a resounding defeat.

The Glendalough Tower was built by a demon at the command of St Kevin. This saint had struck fear into Satan on a previous occasion, so the arch-fiend kept a good distance from the holy place.

Monasterboice was built by a woman under extraordinary circumstances. According to legend, she was young, beautiful and good, but she was persecuted by the senior chieftain. He must have had a bad reputation, for he is portrayed in the story as a ruffian and a villain. The lady pelted her assailant with stones from the safety of the tower. Her heroism was rewarded by her deliverance, for her lover, hearing of the desperate situation, came to her aid and put her besiegers to flight. She was saved, crying out, "Glory be to God!"

Chapter 4

Armagh

The cathedral city of Armagh is situated some fifteen miles south of Lough Neagh, or the Great Lake as the early inhabitants called it. The journey south from the shores of the lake was undertaken at first by foot and horse to the slight height where the present city now stands. The land surrounding the city was farmed without enclosure into the Middle Ages. The road from Lough Neagh was a dirt track until the modern age.

Many travellers came to Armagh as pilgrims, for it was here that St Patrick built his great church, obtaining land from the local chief, Lord Daere.

The population of Armagh before the coming of the Norsemen was very small, but with the coming of the barbarians the Christian city or monastery grew to perhaps 1,000. There were little huts surrounding the site where the Christians worshipped Christ and the Virgin Mary.

To the south-east of Armagh lie the Mountains of Mourne, where St Patrick established his first church at Saul. Thus the first Christian church in Ireland was established.

To the north-west of Armagh rise the less spectacular Sperrin Mountains, famous for their forests, which were still thickly forested in Hugh O'Neill's time (the sixteenth century). The Vikings do not seem to have been interested in the Sperrins, for these mountains were not noted for their agricultural potential. The Sperrins were inhabited by small bands of Gaels, whilst the Norsemen settled and conquered the less high ground around the cathedral city.

The Norsemen also settled in the area of Lough Foyle and Lough Swilly in County Donegal, and the Annals record fierce battles between Viking forces on these waters. There were also battles on Lough Neagh, but few details are known.

The Gaels, of course, hated the Vikings, and they tried to raise armies to deal with the conquerors – but to no avail. The Norsemen had armour and metal swords, whilst the Gaels fought in linen tunics and defended themselves with stone swords.

Directly north of Lough Neagh, the North Antrim Plateau sweeps down to the North Channel, or the Sea of Moyle. Here men may first have come to Ulster in wooden boats, perhaps about 7500 BC. Today the North Channel boasts the Giant's Causeway, geologically unchanged since that time. The pagans put the phenomenon of the causeway down to supernatural forces. I have been there on a number of occasions, enjoying the spectacular scenery.

West of the River Bann lies the Antrim coast, where a coast road was built to open up the Glens of Antrim in the early nineteenth century. From here early settlers travelled to the Antrim area, and later, in the early eighth century, the Vikings came, carrying their longships across the land. Today visitors come to Armagh to look at the two cathedrals, both dedicated to St Patrick, one Protestant (Anglican) and the other Roman Catholic. Today Armagh is the seat of the Church in Ireland, and a tour of the cathedrals is worthwhile, for it puts one in the presence of God. The Anglican cathedral is the oldest, and it looks back on a monastic tradition that began with St Patrick's arrival in the region.

Armagh is a thriving town with a large Protestant population. The coming of the Church to Armagh in the fifth century was a great event for Ireland. Today Protestants and Catholics look back upon a great tradition, albeit in modern times a divided one.

The Queen of the Golden Hair, Macha, is one of the few women that feature in ancient and medieval Irish literature. She was perhaps originally a pagan goddess. Her fortress is said to have lain to the west of the city at Emain Macha. All that remains of the city today is a small hill. Emain Macha was perhaps well known throughout ancient Europe, but, like the rest of Europe, it was overshadowed by ancient and medieval Rome.

The Roman Empire never conquered Ireland, but the men of Armagh must have lived in fear of an invasion from the mainland.

Ulster in pre-Christian times was divided between many different tribes. In the entire island of Ireland the number has been estimated at 250, of which fifty or more might have been in Ulster. Dalriada was an important settlement on the north-east coast of Ulster, Dunseverick was the maritime capital, and it is thought that Ballymoney was the political capital. The two Dalriadas, on opposite sides of the North Channel, carried on good relations with each other.

The union between the Scottish and Irish Dalriadas lasted for many centuries, and its highlight was the founding by St Columba of the monastery of Iona. St Columba was banished from Ireland for political reasons, so he took his curragh and followers to this island of Iona in the Western Isles of Scotland.

The Red Branch Knights of Emain Macha had their headquarters at Armagh, and they rode to many kingdoms in Ulster, asserting their authority. Their numbers were perhaps not large, but Christianity at Armagh was soon firmly established.

Armagh is perhaps the oldest settlement in Ireland, and it owes its existence to the mushrooming of the Church in the fifth century.

Why the Vikings chose an inland site for their activities is not known, but they also colonized centres along the coast, particularly in the Ballycastle region. From their headquarters at York, the Norsemen sailed across the Irish Sea to establish themselves at Dublin. Likewise they also sailed up Belfast Lough, settling perhaps at Carrickfergus after their arrival at Larne Lough. The ancient civilization of Ulster was almost entirely destroyed by the Viking incursions. Dublin, however, survived, along with Armagh, and in the Viking Age they formed the 'capitals' of Ireland.

Chapter 5

Bards

Nicknames were quite common in ancient Ireland. The son of Olaf the White was called Thorstein the Red. Surnames did not exist. Two kings of Norway were Harald Bluetooth and Harold Fairhair. Ivar the Boneless was a warrior that became King of the Dublin Danes. A man called Niall Black Knee was High King of the Gaels, who also sometimes used nicknames.

The common people loved to hear tales of great men. The Irish had their bards, and the Norsemen had storytellers called skalds. The Irish and the Norsemen had much in common, for both told their history in poems which were recited for generation after generation.

The Gaelic monks eventually taught the Norsemen how to read and write, so they started to write down their histories, but the first warriors that came to Ireland could not read or write; so their skalds were very important to them.

The skalds told sagas, which were adventure stories about kings and heroes, many of which were in the form of poems and included real historical events. The Eddas began with the creation of the world. According to the Norsemen, in the beginning there was no heaven and earth. Ymir, the frost giant, was born of vapour. The god Odin and his two brothers killed Ymir and created the earth from his body. They used Ymir's eyebrows to create a place called Midgard, or Middle Earth. Odin made a man out of a tree and a woman out of an alder and he gave them Midgard to live in.

The Vikings believed that a giant ash tree called Yggdrasil held up the universe and that one of its roots reached into Asgard, where the gods lived. The only road to Asgard was a bridge in the form of a rainbow.

The most well known of the palaces of Asgard was the great hall of Valhalla, were Odin lived with his wife, Frigga. Odin was called All-Father and he ruled the other gods in the same way as the High King of Ireland ruled the provincial kings. Odin's son Thor was the strongest of the gods. He was the god of the land and physical power, which was very important in the Viking Age. When they sailed to other shores the Vikings carried Thor's name with them as well as adding 'Thor' to their own personal names.

St Flannan's Cathedral in County Clare has an important ogham stone dating from about AD 1000. One side of the stone reads, 'Thorgrim carved this cross'. On the other side is another inscription: 'A blessing on Thorgrim'. Thorgrim was presumably Christian – one of many Norsemen in Ulster who had converted to Christianity by the eleveneeth century.

When the Norsemen first arrived in Ulster they worshipped many gods and goddesses, each one representing an aspect of life. Frey was the god of rain and sunshine and the fruits of the earth; his sister, Freya, Thor's wife, was the goddess of music and flowers; Bragi was the god of poetry; and Balder was the god of beauty. Viking gods were not gentle – they tended to be aggressive, like the people who worshipped them.

Loki was the good-looking but evil god of mischief – a giant that could change sex and shape. He caused Balder's death.

The Annals contain many tales of battles between the gods,

who fought like mortals and could also die like mortals in certain circumstances.

Some of the names of the week are named after Norse gods: Thursday is Thor's day; Friday is Frey's day; and Wednesday is Woden's day (Odin was also known as Woden).

The Valkyries were the daughters of Odin – warrior women, whose job it was to collect heroes killed in combat and to carry them straight to Valhalla on beautiful warhorses. These horses could gallop through the clouds. Every Norseman hoped to die in battle.

The best known Valkyrie was Brünnhilde. She fell in love with a hero called Siegfried, who had been raised in a forest by a dwarf called Mime. Brünnhilde was the eldest of the Valkyries, and her father's favourite daughter. Fearing that someone might try to take her away from him, Odin encircled Brünnhilde with a ring of magic fire to protect her. But Siegfried broke through and claimed her. They were in love, and, by magic, Brünnhilde made Siegfried invulnerable.

The anger of the gods pursued them, and Siegfried was tricked into forgetting Brünnhilde and marrying someone else. She thought he had deliberately betrayed her. When he was slain, she realized they had both been deceived. In her grief, she destroyed Valhalla.

Another Norse myth predicted the destruction of Valhalla and the end of the world. This is called Ragnarök 'the twilight of the gods'. Ragnarök, it was said, would follow a rough winter, during which snow would fall from all parts of the heavens. Three such winters would pass without any summers, and war would prevail everywhere. A serpent would rise from the sea – the magical serpent called Fenris – and he would ravage the land. Loki, the trickster, would lead other gods in an attack on Valhalla. In the battle that followed, both the gods and their enemies would be slain. The sun would fail, the Earth would collapse into the ocean, and time would end.

The Viking way of life was one of aggressive paganism. The Norsemen attacked the monasteries in an effort to abolish Christianity. In the fifth century the Vikings competed with one another in an effort to attack the Church.

In modern terms, all Norse art was applied art, but aspects of Viking ideology may be seen in early Christian art. The evolution of a Norse style of animal ornamentation can help in the dating of objects, and in mapping Viking society and culture. However, it is thought that the Vikings had good taste, despite their pillaging. Animal ornamentation may represent a belief in the totems. It is important to remember that our knowledge of Viking art is generally dependent upon durable objects of metal and stone. Wood and textiles are rarely preserved. Human skin has not survived.

Distinctions between this world and the next were less sharply defined to a Viking than they are to us, and the same applied between themselves and the animal world. According to Viking philosophy, our lives are predetermined; we cannot change our fate. What is important is how we conduct ourselves as we go to meet it.

In Norse mythology there were many classes of supernatural beings. The gods had servants, such as the Valkyries and Odin's raven. There were also giants, dwarfs, elves and ghosts.

At a Danish ring fort in Ulster, wagons were used as a coffin for a woman's body. She was not buried with the customary pair of brooches, but she wore two single rings, and there were many grave goods, including a bowl that once contained fruit, as well as drinking horns and other utensils. There was a locked oak box containing clothes and pottery and a clump of pellets.

In Scandinavia two women were laid out in a burial chamber within the Oseberg ship. The younger woman may have been a princess and the older one her slave. Objects found in the grave suggest two roles: that of a princess and that of a high priestess. These roles may have been combined in one person. Pre-Christian burial rites throughout Scandinavia demanded that the dead were buried or cremated in their clothes, along with personal ornaments, and a selection of everyday tools. The intention seems to have been to equip the dead for the next world.

Odin required slain warriors to be buried with their weapons. The wealthy were accompanied by their horses, dogs and slaves. Wagons or horses were to be used for the journey into the next life. The Vikings brought cremation to Ulster from their homeland.

The majority of pre-Christian religious activity perhaps took place in open spaces and sacred groves. The so-called 'temple' at Old Uppsala has been cited as a large feasting hall in which pagan festivals may have taken place.

Cremation graves were generally clustered around farms. Cremated remains could be buried inside a bag or a pottery or metal vessel, or spread upon the ground. Multiple cremations were common. Bodies might be placed directly into the ground, or in a coffin, a chamber or a vehicle.

The majority of burials were poorly furnished. Ninth-century burials are the simplest, and the knife is the most common find in graves, whether the body is male or female.

During the 1980s a large number of structures were found which support the theory of small-scale votive activities carried out at special sites. Excavation on the highest point of the island of Frösön in Sweden, under the floor of a medieval church, have uncovered what appear to be the remains of a sacrificial grove. Under the medieval altar were the remains of a birch tree. Around its roots was a large animal-bone assemblage. The stone church was built by the end of the twelfth century.

At another site in Sweden, a cult building was attached to the chieftain's farmstead. The building came into use at the end of the eighth century although much of the ritual belonged to the tenth century. It comprised two rooms separated by a passage. Along the eastern wall there was a stone platform, upon which idols were placed. Two rings were discovered in the south-west part of the house, but there were no other finds. The surrounding ground surface was covered in large stone rings. A large quantity of animal bones were discovered. The rings appear to have carried implements such as hammers and axes, which are usually found singularly in graves. Some were unfinished. Three adjacent buildings with sand floors had been used for metal-working. The animal bones included a high proportion of jaws and skulls – perhaps left over from sacrificial meals – and the remains of a large number of horses, dogs and wolves. There were smaller numbers of cats, beavers, badgers, foxes, red deer and geese.

When Norseman came into close contact with Christians, gradually the Norse beliefs began to be supplanted by Christianity. At first conversion to Christianity only took place under royal approval, but over a period of centuries faith in the old gods vanished.

The initial conversions were made by Christian missionaries. In the early eighth century, Willibrord, an English monk working in Frisia, sailed to Ribe in Denmark, where, according to Alcuin, he was welcomed at the court of King Ongendus, but he made little progress and sailed back to Frisia with thirty boys to instruct in missionary work.

Christian objects found in graves in Scandinavia have often been regarded as loot rather than evidence that the buried person was a Christian. These include over thirty crucifix-shaped pendants. Vessels were frequently decorated with silver-foil crosses, and they have been associated with Christian rites. Possibly they were used for wine.

Women played an important role in pre-Christian Scandinavia, but it has been suggested that conversion was a disaster for women. There were no Christian goddesses and religious practice was officiated entirely by men. Some aspects of the Church, however, would have been attractive to them, including the prohibition of infanticide, the equality of the sexes before God, and belief in a paradise from which women were not excluded. In the Norse tradition, women had a key role in dedicating rune stones.

The decline in Norse beliefs is reflected in the fact that fewer and fewer burials included grave goods. There was a decrease in grave goods by the tenth century. A Danish grave from this period was excavated in Mammen in 1868, and here the grave goods included a gaming board and a silver-inlaid axe, but there were no other weapons. A large candle had been placed in the burial chamber.

Cremation was prohibited by the early Church as it was considered to be a pagan practice; it declined in many places during the tenth century. The remains of as many as seventy bodies were sometimes buried together, and the majority of these cemeteries are from the period between 800 and 1150. During the ninth and early tenth centuries all Norse graves were cremation graves, but by about 950 inhumations were taking place. These inhumations seem to indicate the introduction of Christian beliefs, though they contained some pagan elements. Grave goods, such as representations of Thor's hammer, amulets and food offerings, were included in the burials. At one site secondary inhumations were inserted around 1100 into a large mid-ninth-century barrow, the earlier cremation layer was placed around the insertions and a keystone was added to the mound. This site was robbed, but a small iron cross was uncovered.

The tenth-century introduction of rune stones provided a new means of remembering the dead. There are hundreds of Viking Age runic inscriptions in Sweden, about 250 in Denmark and sixty-five in Norway. The dating of the rune stones emphasizes the long-drawn-out process of Christianization. The earliest Scandinavian churches date from the late tenth century. These churches appear to have started off as chapels built of timber on private estates in the tenth century. A mushrooming of church buildings followed in the twelfth century.

Chapter 6

Viking Gifts

The Norsemen brought more to Ireland than terrorism and surprise raids. They introduced towns and established trade with Europe. Ireland was no longer as isolated as it had been before.

Centuries earlier, Irish monks had travelled east to take the torch of literacy back to Europe after the Dark Ages. They were, however, involved with schools of learning rather than with the wider world of commerce. Traders were engaged in the hard life of buying and selling, travelling extensively, and meeting people who knew nothing about Ulster. The Vikings appreciated the quality of Irish craftsmanship. As well as this, the Norsemen brought something to Ulster that would have a dramatic effect on Irish culture.

Until the arrival of the Vikings, art in Ulster was comprised of abstract symbols and interlaced designs – the legacy of the early Gaels. However, there was another artistic inheritance of the early Gaels. The pagan Gaels believed that the soul resided in the head, and they took human heads as trophies after battles. Their Christian Gaelic descendants decorated their churches with carved stone heads.

Stonemasons and other craftsmen were valued members of the Ulster community; the Gaels were very fond of ornamentation and bright colours. Simple objects, like iron door hinges, were beautifully shaped and decorated with Celtic patterns. Smiths, woodcarvers and other artisans spend their time creating objects of great beauty, and they were an important part of everyday life, but, with the arrival of the Vikings in Ulster, Irish artisans started to be influenced by Norse designs. The Norsemen used animal figures to decorate their ships, weapons and jewellery. Dragons and serpents were popular motifs, and soon dragons started to appear on ornaments throughout Ireland. There were, of course, no snakes in Ireland, but serpents became a part of many Gaelic interlacing designs. Other figures, such as birds and horses, werc slowly introduced into the illuminated manuscripts. To the carved human heads that graced buildings, the Gaels now added carved animal heads.

Viking art was originally German in origin, foi the Norsemen came from the same routes as the Anglo-Saxons. Because the Norsemen travelled so widely, they added elements from other cultures, copying lions from late Roman belt fittings.

Their portrayals of animals were not very realistic. Sometimes one creature flowed into another, and many of the figures had only a head, neck and forelimbs. However, they all had one thing in common: vitality. Norse art, like the people themselves, was full of energy.

Irish art also influenced the Vikings. The Norse women started to dress like the Irishwomen. A common gown style was one of pleated linen; the more pleats there were, the finer the gown. Some of these gowns had short sleeves, whilst others had no sleeves and were fastened at the throat by ribbons. Over this the women wore a linen tunic held by a brooch. The design on the brooches was by now a blend of Celtic interlaced and Norse animal forms.

By the late tenth century, it would have been difficult to distinguish a Norse from a Gael. Even the weapons the warriors carried were becoming more similar. When the Gaels started to use the axe, they proved themselves adept at it. They were also not slow to strip Viking bodies on the battlefield for their armour.

It became important for each band of warriors to have a banner to follow, to avoid confusing one side with the other on the battlefield.

The Norse smith kept his forge glowing into the night, as there was in Ulster a demand for new weapons. Ulster was at the heart of an expanding Norse kingdom. Traders brought the smiths raw metal to be shaped into swords, daggers and axes, to beat back the Gaels and to repulse the Danes.

The hilts of the swords and daggers were beautifully carved. A favourite design featured a number of unusual animals, none of them recognizable.

In some cases, the smith's wife was a skilled artisan too, and it was she that made the scabbards, cutting Viking designs deep into the leather. Such weapons were highly prized and sold for high prices. When blades were broken in battle, the smiths would melt them down and reforge them, for metal was too valuable to waste.

In addition to new art forms, the Vikings brought Norse ponies into Ireland. The Gaels already had some horses, but the animals were not native to Ireland, and it is believed that they came to the island with the early Celts. Norse ponies brought fresh blood. They were small and hardy and could get by with little food. The Norse, however, did not use these horses as warhorses. Like the Gaels, they preferred to fight on foot. The ponies of course were a valuable means of transportation, both for riding and for drawing carts.

The Irish (who loved horses) traded with the Vikings for their ponies. Trade increased, and the more goods were brought into Ireland the more the Gaels coveted them.

In order to carry on trade, people had to have a common language. The Norsemen tried to learn Irish, but the Gaels were also borrowing words and learning to speak the Norse language.

The Vikings and the Irish were drawing closer together, but the Norsemen were still invaders, and every new dragon ship on the sea heralded more of the invaders.

One can imagine fleets of seven or eight longships arriving in the sheltered waters of Larne Lough after several days' sailing from Rathlin Island. They would have rowed past the present-day Maidens lighthouses, which lie five miles off the Antrim coast. Today there is a good view of the lighthouses from Drains Bay.

Chapter 7

Norse Life in Ulster

As more Vikings arrived in Ireland, they built more towns for themselves where they could carry on trade. As a result many places in Ulster today have Norse names – Carlingford and Strangford, for example. In the south of Ireland there are many others.

While the Gaels lived on scattered farmsteads, the Norsemen built their houses close together, with narrow lanes between them. These houses were built of local materials – wattle and daub, and timber. Some of the earliest of them were triangular in shape, as was the custom in the Scandinavian lands, and they looked like upended Viking boats. As time went by, Gaelic methods of construction became more popular.

Posts were set in the floor to support a thatched roof and to help divide interior spaces. There were stone-hearthed fireplaces in the centre, but no chimneys, so the smoke had to escape through doors and windows. Benches along the walls served as beds. In more-wealthy homes private chambers were sometimes set aside and provided with separate doorways. Wattle was used for floor mats. In the main streets, wattle was even laid down on top of wooden pathways, which kept people out of the thick mud and mire.

Close to the docks in every Viking coastal town, a number of businesses sprang up – carpenters, shipwrights, coopers, smiths, other craftsmen and merchants made the air ring with noise from before dawn until after dark in both summer and winter. As the towns grew, houses were torn down so that bigger houses could be built on their sites.

Viking settlements had no sewage systems. Waste was simply thrown into the streets, which soon became miry and foul. Rotting rubbish was piled into open middens, which were a breeding ground for flies. River mud, smoked fish, wet wool and unwashed bodies all added to the stench of the Viking towns. The Vikings were well used to this, and perhaps did not take much notice. This may be the reason why the Gaels preferred to remain country-dwellers, leaving the towns to the Vikings.

There was a Norse settlement at Limerick, on the Shannon estuary. Arriving as raiders, the Vikings plundered an island in the River Shannon as early as the year 812. They stayed in the area to build a trading base with easy access to the sea.

The Norsemen slept in their clothes, which provided them with warmth. An Ulster Viking would wear a knee-length woollen tunic, tied at the waist, with long sleeves and loosely fitted trousers of wool. All the Vikings' clothes were made by the women, who also spun the wool and dyed the fabric.

In Norse houses, wooden benches lined the walls. The family ate their meals on the benches and slept under them at night, using straw pallets laid on the earth floor. The interior of the house was very cluttered. As well as a fire in the centre of the house, there would have been a loom, many pots and cauldrons, tools, ropes, closets, chests for clothing and supplies, baskets and casks.

Norse wives at this time wore woollen gowns with full

sleeves, a high neck and a large skirt that reached to the tops of their leather shoes. The cloth was dyed with woad, madder, onion skins and berries. Over her gown, a woman would wear an apron consisting of two panels (one in the front and another at the back), reaching to her knees. The panels were joined across the shoulders by a strap held in place with oval brooches. Another brooch was fitted with small chains, holding the family's keys, shears and other small necessities. Women dressed their hair in the Norse fashion: they wound it around their head, then covered it with a napkin knotted behind their ears. They wore necklaces of coloured glass beads, perhaps set with a few precious silver balls.

It was Norse custom to eat a large meal first thing in the morning. This might consist of porridge, soft cheese, herrings and some dried mutton.

Norse children did not attend school. Like their parents, they could not read or write, but they were well educated for the sort of lives they were expected to lead. Boys were trained by their fathers to follow the sea or to learn a trade. Girls learned cooking, sewing and weaving from their mothers. All the children were expected to help with the household chores. These included chopping wood for the fire, carrying water, carding wool for the loom, minding vats of dye, churning butter, milking goats and performing simple repairs about the house.

The children were kept busy most of the day, but they had a little time for play. Their fathers carved wooden toys for them. They also liked to play at war, with a lot of shouting and running about. A man would never venture outside without a weapon in his belt.

A market area in the centre of the town would contain shops and stalls, pens for livestock and perhaps even slaves. The Norsemen captured Gaelic children and sold them on their excursions abroad. Irish children were considered very beautiful, with their white skin and fine features. Young

Irishwomen fetched high prices in the Mediterranean slave markets.

Towns were often built at the mouths of rivers – for example, the River Bann and the River Foyle both had Viking settlements where they meet the sea. Larne is also at the mouth of a river.

The Gaels frequently brought goods to these towns to trade with the Vikings, and the Vikings sailed up the rivers to plunder the tribes who dwelt on their banks. The rivers of Ulster were like a vast highway system.

As the Vikings fanned out across the north of Ireland, intermarriage became more common. A hybrid race called the Gall Gaedhil emerged and formed roving bands of raiders, more savage even than the original Norsemen. They often sold their services to the highest bidder.

Intermarriage also had another effect, for some of the Norsemen were converted to Christianity by their Irish wives. For a long time, however, the Vikings were the sworn enemies of the Church.

According to legend, in the ninth century a Norse sea king, Turgesius, attempted to unite all the Vikings in Ireland under his rule and establish paganism throughout the island.

Among the Vikings, the priesthood was not a separate class. Instead the head of the family was also its priest, and sacrifices were offered to the gods.

Three times in one month Turgesius attacked Armagh, the ecclesiastical centre of the island, but he failed to destroy the church in Ireland. He was at length taken prisoner by the High King of Ireland, and he was drowned as a punishment for his crimes. However, as a result of the growing colonization by the Norse, some of the Gaels reverted to paganism, and amongst these were many of the Gall Gaedhil.

The Danes of Dublin were the first to embrace Christianity. Their conversion was perhaps partly due to their extensive trade with the Anglo-Saxons, who were also Christians. The Christian Gaels of Dublin marked themselves with a cross, as did the entire Christian population of Ulster. They said they followed the White Christ.

The Norsemen also introduced their own system of government into their settlements. In the north of Ireland most of the towns had a 'thing', where the people assembled once a year to enact laws, pass judgements and elect officials. All were welcome to attend. The Norse system of government was much fairer than the Gaelic system.

The Vikings in Ulster remained divided. Danish settlements, such as Larne, Armagh and Derry, had strong ties with other Danish settlements in the south of Ireland – particularly in Limerick. Larne became a major trading centre and did much trade with the west of Scotland. There was an extensive slave trade at Larne.

More and more Viking habits started to appear in Irish life. Gaelic food and clothing were influenced by Norse styles, and new techniques were introduced in baking, brewing and weaving. Danish ale became a popular refreshment, almost replacing buttermilk.

Although the Vikings were becoming permanent settlers in Ireland, their dependence upon the longships remained. They continued to build vessels in the traditional way, with a dragon-headed prow and a graceful curve rising at the stern.

Shipbuilding took place in the open. The keel was laid first, and it was cut and shaped from a single huge tree, usually oak. Irish oak was ideal for this purpose. Once the keel was ready, a level base was prepared by splitting logs and fashioning planking from them. Each layer of planking was called a strake and was fastened to the keel with iron nails. Overlapping strakes were caulked with pitch and animal hair to keep the ship watertight. The angle at which the strakes were fastened determined the shape of the ship. Once the straking was in place, internal support timbers were added. Floor timbers were fastened to these, held in place by means of wooden pegs. Cross-beams were set across the ends of the floor timbers.

A keelson was fitted on top of the keel to secure the mast. This was supported by another cross-beam, which also served as a rowing bench. If there was to be a cargo hold, a gap was left amidships.

Once the mast was put into place, the rigging and other fittings were added. The longships had a square loose-fitting sail, and they carried a row of shields along the gunwales.

Not all ships were used for raiding on the open sea. Some were coasters, never sailing out of sight of the land. Smaller ships were designed to be used on rivers.

Every Norse vessel was strong as well as graceful, and all were capable of great speed, either under sail or driven by oars. The longships brought prosperity and power to Ireland, and they thought both would last for ever.

Chapter 8

An Age of Transformation

From 875 until 914, more hordes of Norsemen invaded Ulster. The Vikings in Ireland were already established in their towns, and their main interest was now trading. They did a little local raiding, but they did not try to expand their territory. This was perhaps a period of peace, but the Gaels still fought amongst themselves. In the tenth century events in the north and south took separate courses. Munster had become a battleground for Gaelic chieftains fighting for control of the province. The Eóganacht dynasty was fighting the Dal Cais for supremacy. At length the Eóganacht chieftain won control of Munster, claiming the kingship of Cashel in 954. He opposed the Vikings of Limerick, but he at last entered into a trading relationship with them. They settled in an uneasy peace. The chieftain allowed the Vikings to tax the local Irish very heavily, and he took a share for himself, which caused more trouble in Munster.

More Vikings arrived. A fresh wave of raids took place, using both sea-going longships and riverboats in large numbers.

The air rang with the clash of axes and swords. A map of Ulster at this time shows battlefields and military quarters from one end of the province to the other.

Niall Black Knee, the High King, waged a campaign against the Vikings, and he urged many of the Ulster chieftains to unite and stand with him. While Munster was torn by feuds, Ulster began to unite against the Norsemen. The Vikings were well established throughout the British Isles. They had overrun England, whose great king, Alfred, had been able to secure only one-third of his country against the foreigners. By now the Vikings had reached Spain and Italy and had opened up trading relations with what is modern-day Istanbul. By 913 they had 500 ships in the Caspian Sea, and they were doing much trade in Russian furs, Greek and Arabian silks, and Indian spices. Many of these luxuries found their way to Ulster, where the kings and chieftains had developed a taste for silk and cinnamon.

To chase the Vikings out of Ulster would have meant a loss in material goods that not all the Gaels were willing to suffer. The northern kings who stood with Niall Black Knee were willing to make sacrifices. At first their united armies had much success and it looked as if Norse trading might be affected.

In 918 a large fleet of longships arrived at Dublin Bay, and at the same time the Vikings set up a camp near present-day Rathfarnham. Niall and his warriors suffered a resounding defeat. He and many of his allies were killed, leaving the Norse triumphant.

Ulster watched as the Dublin Vikings undertook a campaign that started with the destruction of the church at Kells and the massacre of martyrs there in 920. Shortly after this the Danish King of Dublin, Sitric, left the city to take up a kingship at York. He was replaced by his brother.

To celebrate his new kingship, a massive raid was launched against the primatial see at Armagh – another in the long line of raids. He had planned the raid for early November, the feast of St Martin, when Armagh was crammed with pilgrims.

The Norsemen fell upon the city and sacked it, seizing a fortune in loot. They then divided their forces to pillage the countryside for miles around. One large body of warriors went east, another went west, and the others went north along the Blackwater river. At the end of the day the Irish counterattacked and were victorious. They routed the Norsemen, who fled in the dusk. A treasure trove of Viking axe heads was abandoned along the way of their flight as the Vikings were hunted down.

In 941 a Gael undertook a project so dangerous that it earned him great fame and a unique nickname. At that time Donagh was High King of Ireland, and Muirchertach hoped to become High King when he died. He assembled 1,000 hand-picked warriors and equipped them with specially made cloaks of tanned leather. Then they set off in a circuit of all Ireland. Wherever he went he bestowed lavish gifts and behaved in a most kingly fashion. Such a circuit had never been made before by any but a High King. Muirchertach was bold and brave, and soon all Ulster was talking about him. They called him Muirchertach of the Leather Cloaks. A poet described his cloak as his house and shelter. They were aroused by music; and as they danced the shaking of their leather cloaks could be heard.

When Muirchertach reached Dublin he pitched camp, demanding food and spoils of war from the local Norsemen. He took the King of Dublin as a hostage and entertained him in royal fashion for some months before turning him over to Donagh. This gesture was to be his last. In March 943, while Donagh still lived, Muirchertach was killed in battle.

So the wars went on, year after year, and it looked as if no one would ever stop them. However, not everyone hated the Vikings. The Gaels had developed a taste for their goods, and they accepted them as a permanent part of their way of life. As a result of intermarriage, the divisions between the Vikings and the Gaels was becoming blurred.

Dublin remained to a large extent a city of foreigners. The only Irish within the walls of Dublin were slaves. Danish Dublin would remain an alien settlement, in thought and tradition, based on international trade and looking upon the rest of Ireland as a place to plunder.

Chapter 9

Olaf of the Shoes

In 975 Olaf Cuaran was a contented man. Although he was not a young man, he had a young wife – a princess of Leinster called Gormlaith. He was also King of Dublin. Dublin had been rebuilt after one of its many burnings, and a new timber palisade now surrounded the entire town. Watchtowers had been built at intervals, and the riverbanks had been reinforced with stone and planking to protect the city from flooding.

Dublin harbour attracted more trading vessels from Ulster, bringing more and more interesting cargo to the city and port. Irish leather was an important part of Dublin's export trade, of which Olaf claimed a percentage. Ulstermen travelled to the port to stock up with goods to bring north to the Gaelic settlements. The city was sometimes besieged, but Olaf did not let it worry him much.

For centuries, Ulster chiefs had battered their way into Dublin, set fire to buildings, grabbed what loot they could, and then retreated into the dense forests and lakelands, but the Vikings remained in control of the city. The Gaels were not interested in taking and keeping towns.

According to the Irish Annals, Olaf Cuaran was a Christian.

The Norsemen were now being converted to the faith of the Gaels. By around 930, the city that Olaf ruled had timber churches where Christ was worshipped instead of Thor and Odin, but the Dubliners were still Norse at heart.

In 979 a prince of the Uí Neill tribe of Ulster, called Malachi, defeated an army of Vikings in a battle near Tara. By the following year Malachi was High King of Ireland.

Olaf Cuaran was not alarmed, for he expected that Malachi would quieten down now that his rule was firmly established, and the other kings paid Olaf's taxes without too much trouble. He thought Malachi would retire to his headquarters at Tara to enjoy his spoils. This had been the habit of the High Kings for some time, and Olaf Cuaran did not think it would change.

However, as soon as Malachi was made High King, he marched on Dublin, and, following a siege that lasted for only three days, he took the city, took much plunder and freed 2,000 Irish captives. Malachi issued a famous proclamation, which read that every one of the Gaels who were in the territory of the Gaels should go to their own territory in peace and happiness. Malachi asserted that he now considered Dublin to be under his rule, and he demanded that the king of the Dublin Danes should bend his knee to him. It was a situation that no Viking could tolerate.

However, Olaf Cuaran was not a young man, and he no longer thirsted after battle. Life with his wife was not easy, for she was demanding and had a fierce temper. Olaf of the Shoes was now becoming tired. His head ached when he went to bed at night and his body ached in the morning. Food did not taste good to him. His eyes were dim and his hearing was failing. Life, and the kingship of Dublin, was becoming a burden. But he was a Viking and he could not run away from battle.

Then, to the surprise of everyone, he announced that he was becoming a Christian and that he intended to go on pilgrimage to Iona in the Western Isles. He might be there for some time, he said. He put his wife in the charge of the Dublin Danes along with his young son Sitric until he returned.

Olaf was a shrewd man and he did not think Malachi (who by now was calling himself Malachi Mor (Malachi the Great) would attack an Irish princess and her little boy. The main reason he was heading for Scotland was because of his demanding wife.

Olaf died on Iona, and Gormlaith, his widow, surprised everyone by marrying Malachi Mor. Sitric was proclaimed king of the Dublin Danes.

As far as Dublin was concerned, Sitric was not a bad king. When he grew up, he proved to be a worthy leader. He was as shrewd and ambitious as his mother. He caused the first coins to be minted in Ireland, and his own image was stamped on them. At length coins would replace cattle as a means of exchange. In some ways Malachi Mor and Sitric were unlucky, for in the west a man was coming to power who would surpass both of them. His name was Brian Boru.

Chapter 10

Brian Boru and the Battle of Clontarf

Long before he became High King of Ireland, Brian Boru had battled with the Norsemen. When he was a lad in Thomond (County Clare), the Norsemen of Limerick plundered up and down the River Shannon. They came out of the mist, and he never forgot the ferocity of the attack on the ring fort where he lived, the smell of the flames and smoke, the smell of burning timbers. Throughout his life he would remember the sight of the dead bodies. In the remains of his home, the little boy who was Brian Boru wept, for his heart had been broken.

After his mother's death, life changed for young Brian. He was educated in the monastic schools at Clonmacnoise and Innisfallen, where he learned to read and write Latin and Greek. He also studied the lives of great men, such as Alexander the Great, Julius Caesar and the Emperor Charlemagne. From reading about their campaigns, he developed ideas of his own about warfare.

When Brian's brother, Mahon, became King of Munster, he eventually made a treaty with Ivar, the Norse King of Limerick, but Brian waged guerrilla warfare against the Norsemen. He was familiar with every inch of the mountains of Thomond and its dense forests of oak, yew and fir. With a small band of warriors, he lured many Vikings to their deaths. As he matured he became one of the most skilled warriors Ireland has ever produced.

At last he left the wilderness and joined Mahon at Cashel, the seat of the Munster kings. He became a leader in Mahon's army of Munster men. The Norsemen broke their treaty with Brian's brother, and Brian defeated them in the Battle of Sulcoit. He followed them back to Limerick, where he found a large number of enslaved Irish children. He was so angry that he executed 3,000 Norse in revenge.

When Mahon was assassinated by an Eóganacht chieftain, Brian Boru became King of Munster. He now put some of his ideas into practice. He introduced the idea of disciplined cavalry and formed the first Irish navy. At one time he had 300 boats anchored on the River Shannon, as well as others in Ulster. He also built for himself a great stronghold called Ceann Coradh, near what is now the town of Killaloe.

Meanwhile Brian continued to fight the Norsemen. He wanted to drive them out of Ireland. As he aged, his attitude, however, changed. He took a Norse boy as a foster-son, and he even recruited Norse warriors into the Munster armies. He turned his eyes towards Tara, the residence of the High Kings of Ireland.

Malachi Mor, Brian realized, was not a great leader. During his reign Ireland was divided, and bedevilled by outlaws. Malachi was unable to bring peace, even within his own family, and he fought constantly with his wife, Gormlaith, until he finally 'set her aside' – the term for divorce under Brehon Law.

Brian decided that someone else should be High King. According to tradition, Brian himself was ineligible. The title was always held by a member of the powerful Uí Neill tribe of Ulster, but Brian was a member of the Dal Cais. However, he was powerful, and he had earned a great reputation as a fighting man. He had won the support of numerous tribal kings and he knew how to play politics. He also had a vision of the future.

By the time he challenged Malachi for the High Kingship, Brian had accepted the fact that the Vikings could not be driven out of Ireland. By this time they had been there for 200 years; they had married Irishwomen, built towns and established trade. The Vikings were now part of Ireland.

Brian set about winning them over. He married one of his daughters to Sitric Silkbeard, and he encouraged the Norse to start to think of themselves as Gaels.

He also had another surprise in store. Brian Boru married Sitric's mother, Gormlaith, the Gael princess who had been married to the King of Dublin and to the High King of Ireland. Such a wife was a symbol of his great power.

Eventually Brian defeated Malachi Mor and became High King in 1002. He at once tried to unify the island. This was not an easy matter, and it had never been thought possible, but Brian was a cunning king. Step by step he won over the many kings and chiefs – some by friendship, others by intimidation. He was a usurper and he had broken all the traditions in his rise to power, but he had obtained the support of the Church by rebuilding churches and monasteries. For example, he laid a gift of twenty ounces of gold at the altar of Armagh Cathedral. He even won the grudging acceptance of the kings and chieftains of Ulster.

From 1002 to 1014 Ireland was at peace. Brian Boru had established such a great reputation that even the Gall Gaedhil obeyed the law. According to a poet of the time, a beautiful woman in all her finery was able to ride the length of the island without being molested.

Unfortunately, the long history of Viking violence had not yet ended. The biggest battle of all had yet to come, and it was to change the course of Irish history.

On Good Friday, 23 April 1014, at Clontarf in the north of

County Dublin, Brian Boru's army met the armies of Sigurd of Orkney; Brodir of the Isle of Man; Sitric Silkbeard, King of Dublin; and Maelmora, King of Leinster. The ancient Irish Annals tell of thousands of Norsemen, including 1,000 covered in chain mail from head to foot. Many of the great warriors of Ulster came at the invitation of Brian's son-in-law Sitric and his treacherous Gael ally Maelmora. Maelmora was a brother of Gormlaith.

Brian, like Olaf and Malachi before him, had divorced Gormlaith, and as a result Sitric and Maelmora vowed to take revenge upon Brian Boru. The divorce was only an excuse. Leinster and Munster were old rivals, and Maelmora had always hated Brian. Neither he nor Sitric liked Brian's policies and they did not want peace. They wanted to revert to the old ways, which were more rewarding.

Sitric and Maelmora wanted Brian dead so that they could divide Ireland between them. They had summoned all the other Vikings to come to Ireland to help them defeat the High King. Many had gladly replied.

Brian was now seventy-three years of age, and he had to fight for Ireland one more time. With him were his eldest son, Murrough, together with many other Gaelic kings and Brian's Norse allies.

It was not simply the Gaels against the Norse at Clontarf – it was the Gaels and the Vikings against the Irish. Warriors on both sides wielded battleaxes.

Hundreds of longships from Norway, Sweden and Denmark arrived in force in Dublin Bay from Orkney and the Isle of Man. From the walls of Dublin, the masts of the ships looked like a forest rising out of the sea.

Brian Boru camped at what is now Kilmainham the night before the battle, and at dawn he rode out at the head of his forces. Brian wanted to lead his men into battle himself, but because of his age his captains persuaded him to leave the command to his eldest son, Murrough, and to stay behind the battle lines, where they thought he would be safe.

At this time all of Dublin town was situated south of the River Liffey. Only Dubhgall's Bridge connected the town to the spot where the Vikings were landing. Much of the area was covered by a forest known as Tomar's Wood. Here Brian set up his tent so that he could be as close as possible to the battle.

The fighting quickly started, and Brian's own Dal Cais were the first to meet the Vikings. Led by Murrough, they ran forward screaming in fury. The Norsemen replied in kind, and the air rang with the clashing of the swords, the hissing of the spears and the thud of the axes.

Murrough was a fierce warrior, and the Annals tell us he had a sword in both of his hands. He and Sigurd of Orkney fought each other face-to-face. At last Murrough cut the straps of the Viking's helmet with a blow from one of his swords, and killed him with the other.

A great cry rose up from the Norsemen, but the battle was far from over. It spread throughout much of what is now North Dublin. The fiercest fighting took place at Clontarf, where there was a fishing weir on the River Tolka.

Meanwhile Brian Boru waited patiently in his tent. With great concern he sent attendants to see what was happening and to report back to him.

The battle went one way and then the other. It was the bloodiest battle in Irish history, greater than any conflict that has been fought in Ulster, a most warlike province. The Annals tell us of blood dripping from trees in the forest, where the most savage axe fighting took place.

Towards evening the High King's forces finally defeated the Vikings. The Leinstermen and Sitric were slain at Dubhgall's Bridge as they tried to escape to safety within the walls of Dublin.

Some Vikings tried to reach their ships, anchored in the bay, but the tide had turned, and, to their dismay, they found that a great expanse of water now lay between them and their longships. The Irish pursued them and showed no mercy. By the time darkness closed in, Dublin was full of panicky Norsemen. In addition to the thousands who had been slain in battle, many more were drowned as they tried to swim to their longships.

Maelmora was killed and so were most of his chieftains. However, Sitric Silkbeard did not perish because he did not fight: with his mother, Gormlaith, he watched the entire battle from the safety of the walls of Dublin.

Clontarf was an important victory for Brian Boru's armies. The Norsemen were so thoroughly defeated that they now turned their back upon Ireland and concentrated on Britain – the larger island. By the following year, a Dane, Canute, would rule England.

Although the Battle of Clontarf was a triumph for the defenders, Ireland suffered a great loss.

After the battle, Brodir fled into the forest and stumbled across Brian's tent. According to some accounts, he was the final king to die on that day, Good Friday, but the Annals relate that Brodir was captured.

Murrough's fifteen-year-old son, Turlough, was found dead with his fingers still clutching the hair of a slain Norseman. Murrough and most of Brian's other sons also died at Clontarf. When Brian Boru died, there was no man left alive capable of taking his place.

Chapter 11

Brian Boru and the Aftermath of Clontarf

The victory at Clontarf shocked the Vikings The Norse who remained in Ireland (including Ulster) licked their wounds and concentrated on peaceful farming and trade. Without Brian to lead them, the Gaelic kings started to fight amongst themselves again. Malachi was now an old man, and he didn't have the energy to unite Ireland.

In 1035, Sitric Silkbeard, like his father before him, left Dublin to go on pilgrimage. He returned the following year, and gave a grant of treasure and land to build a church (the Church of the Blessed Trinity) on the site of what would become Christ Church Cathedral, Dublin. Towns such as Waterford, Wexford, Carlingford, Limerick and Dublin continued to flourish, and other towns sprang up, but their character changed as more and more Gaels moved into them. By now the cultures of the Norse and the Gaels were starting to merge.

Meanwhile more tribal warfare was taking place, and Norsemen could be found fighting on all sides. The peace that Brian Boru had brought to Ireland was becoming only a memory.

In 1052, Leinster Gaels frequently captured Dublin, but the Danes soon recovered it.

The final Norse raids on Ireland took place in 1102. In that year, Magnus, the King of Norway, sailed into Dublin harbour. He was received by Muirchertach Ua Briain, with a strong army at his back. Magnus organized a truce, and, after spending some time in the city, he sailed peaceably back to Norway. When he returned to Ireland, he was ambushed and killed on the coast of Ulster. He was buried in the cathedral at Downpatrick, out of respect for his position.

In 1170, the Norman invasion of Ireland under the command of Strongbow had started.

Clontarf seemed to signal the end of the Vikings in Ireland, but strangely it was just the beginning. When the Vikings ceased to plunder and pillage, the Norse became a great asset. They built more towns, roads and harbours. They never ceased to expand their network of international trade. Viking ports like Derry and Larne may seem primitive to the modern mind, but through them came Baltic amber, jet and walrus ivory, fine linen, Flemish cloth, wine from Gaul, silk from the East and pottery from the Mediterranean. These commodities enriched the lives of the more prosperous Gaels and gave them a sense of what lay beyond Irish shores.

The Vikings were great travellers, and they brought knowledge of the wider world to Ireland. They also converted to Christianity in great numbers, and many of them became as dedicated to Christ as they had been to Thor. Descendants of the Vikings entered the priesthood; they became monks, nuns and bishops. Armagh looked to the see of Rome for leadership as the Pope prayed for his new flock. They helped to spread the good news to all parts of the world. The Vikings had started as barbarians, but they were not savages. They were hardy, energetic and artistic. They were like the Gaels in some ways. They had forced change upon the Gaels, and much of the change was for good.

Chapter 12

The Vikings in Scotland and Abroad

From earliest times Ulster had close relations with the west of Scotland. The Vikings built upon this. Perhaps before reaching Ulster they made a mark upon the Hebrides, Orkney and Shetland. The Vikings started to conquer the lands of the Picts of Northern Scotland, and at a later date Ulster might have been stepping stone to Scotland. Some historians believe the Norsemen carried out a policy of wholesale genocide. There was large-scale folk migration to the Northern Isles, and small-scale colonization of the Western Isles. The Hebrides may have been repopulated from Ulster during the Middle Ages. The high proportion of Scandinavian ancestry in Orkney and Shetland may point to a long period of close political, economic and social ties with Norway, perhaps starting before the Viking Age. The archaeological evidence points to large-scale migration, followed by Viking political, linguistic and cultural domination.

The Hebrides, as well as being linked with Ulster, were also linked with the Isle of Man as one kingdom under the Lordship of the Isles. They shared a Norse inheritance, including evidence of clinker-built vessels. It has been argued that the linguistic evidence points to a later overlay on an entirely Old Norse-speaking population, although the place names are a mixture of Gaelic and Old Norse.

Much of the archaeological evidence was discovered so long ago that its value is limited. The scene has been dominated by graves – often chance discoveries as a result of the erosion of sand dunes. It is certain that the dead were dressed in full Scandinavian costume and were well equipped with grave goods. At Colonsay and Oronsay they were placed in rowing boats.

The cemetery of a small community has been excavated more recently at Kneep on the Isle of Lewis. It includes men, women and children, some buried with grave goods and some without. A middle-aged woman from the tenth century has been found buried in traditional Norse costume.

As on the Isle of Man it appears that the Hebridean Norse settlers were asserting their cultural identity through an emphasis on Scandinavian dress and custom. Unlike on the Isle of Man, it appears that this strategy embraced wives as well.

Norse settlements have been identified within grass-covered mounds on sand dunes. Recent excavations on North and South Uist tell the same story. At Udal on North Uist Norse longhouses were built, and this must have been the case in Ulster too. These houses were built amongst the ruins of Pictish farms on five settlement mounds. The first structure built by the new occupants there was a defensive enclosure on the highest point of the site.

Fresh Norse styles of pottery, metalwork and combs appear. The introduction of ceramic platters for making barley cakes indicates a change in cuisine as well.

On South Uist, settlement mounds are found.

Although the farms kept their location from prehistoric times, new artefacts and new buildings appeared during the Norse period. At Cille Pheadair a tenth-century timber hall represents a sharp departure from local building tradition. At Bornish, a long-lived Pictish settlement was levelled during the creation of a Norse farmstead. The buildings appear to have existed before the laying of the floor.

By the late eleventh century, Ulstermen were living in a classic Scandinavian style. In Ulster there were substantial stone buildings, copied from the Picts of the north of Scotland. The inhabitants of Ulster were in this period affluent. They were importing pottery from Wessex, and they made antler combs.

In Ulster, houses were rebuilt over earlier structures to provide a link with the past.

The life of Findan, a ninth-century hagiography, is the most important document recording the settlement of Orkney. It provides an historical account of a Gaelic aristocrat's escape from Viking slave traders on Orkney and his subsequent stay with a Bishop, a Pict. This has been dated to about 840.

A Norse saga written between 1192 and 1206 says that Orkney was settled by Earl Ragnald after fleeing from Norway. It gives an interesting picture of life in Norse Orkney in the ninth century.

By the twelfth century, Orkney was a thriving Norse state. It did not become part of Scotland until 1468, when it was signed over to King James III, as part of the dowry of Margaret of Denmark.

There are a few place names that indicate a pre-Norse Pictish population connected with the east coast of what is today County Antrim. Scandinavian names wiped out all but a handful of the indigenous names.

Excavation of a number of sites around the Bay of Birsay indicates a Norse takeover of another power. According to the sagas, Earl Thorfinn had his permanent residence at Birsay, where he worshipped Christ, the new God.

In the second half of the ninth century, Pictish buildings in both Scotland and Ulster were attributed to the Norse. Substantial Norse halls were constructed in Ulster, with wall benches and iron beds. Ironwork was carried on on the island, and silver was melted down. But the community was not self-sufficient, and joints of meat were brought from farms in the bay. Here successive generations of cellular buildings in the Pictish style were replaced by rectangular halls, although Pictish material was still used. At Pool on Sanday, there is a period of overlap between the two cultural groups.

Altogether about 130 sites have been excavated on Orkney. There appears to have been a broader-based settlement here than in the Hebrides, and most remains can be dated to between 850 and 950. The majority were discovered in the nineteenth century, and records of these are poor.

The cemetery at Rousay, however, has been excavated recently. It consisted of thirty-two inhumations, but only eight graves – four male and one female. One grave was of a mother in her twenties, buried with her baby. She had been buried wearing a pair of oval Norse brooches and a string of beads, but she also wore a remarkable silver-and-gold penannular Gaelic brooch. She was a wealthy woman and may have been the head of a family. Two male warriors were buried in little rowing boats. One had probably died in battle, for arrows were lodged in his back. The remainder were buried within graves in stone-lined cists. These graves are perhaps typical of pre-Norse burials. Their position was marked on the surface by boulders, but none had been disturbed by the Norse. On the same promontory there was a boathouse and a farm, comprising a large hall (furnished with wall benches on either side of the hearth) and two byres – one for cattle, one for sheep.

Another discovery was made in 1991. Protruding from a low cliff at Scar, on Sanday, was a small rowing vessel. It had been built in Norway and brought to Orkney in a large boat. A woman in her twenties had been given pride of place in the centre. Her grave goods included a maple-wood box, an iron cooking spit and a fine whalebone plaque of North Norwegian type. She was accompanied by a child aged about ten, and a man in his thirties had been squashed into one end of the boat. It is thought he was not a slave, for he carried a comb, a sword, and some arrows as well as twenty-two whalebone gaming pieces. Carbon dating suggests that a date close to the ninth century obtains, rather than a date in the mid-tenth century. Many of the objects seem to be older, suggesting that they were heirlooms.

At St Magnus, and at Deerness, there are the remains of private stone churches dating to the early tenth century. By the eleventh century, considerable resources were invested in the building of churches throughout Orkney. The remains of these stone buildings underlay the later chapels. There were about 250 burials on the site, including burials under the floor of the churches themselves. Two tenth-century coins were recovered beneath the stone floor.

It has been suggested that survival of 'Papa' place names on Orkney reflects the survival of Pictish Christian enclaves, and perhaps they were responsible for the early conversions of the Vikings.

By 900 the Picts had been overshadowed, politically, linguistically, culturally and socially. The Pictish aristocracy had been overthrown in favour of the Norse, and only at the lower levels of society can evidence of Pictish culture be seen.

Shetland is mentioned somewhat less in the Norse sagas, but it was perhaps colonized at the same time as Orkney, and enjoyed close connections with Norway.

There has been little archaeological evidence of Norse farmsteads in the British Isles.

Norse innovations included the introduction of flax

cultivation, possibly for use in linen manufacture and in fishing nets. Barley and oats were grown.

On the small island of Uist, Stefan Strumann has sought to map the Norse landscape. Uist is now largely depopulated, with a present population of 600 people, but the remains of Norse buildings have been recorded at thirty places. These sites have proved difficult to date. A small number of burial sites on Uist have yielded ninth-century finds. The settlements may have started in that period, but some are long-lived and continued in use until the fourteenth and fifteenth centuries. Most comprise typical Viking longhouses, with wall benches and central hearths. Soapstone vessels are among the commonest finds.

Shetland was treeless, and the timbers for the main structural beams must have been imported. At Underhoull a bow-sided hall was built with footings from stone. There is an Iron Age broch and other Pictish structures. The use of timber was extravagant for the construction of the Norse longhouses, whereas Pictish architecture tended to make use of stone rather than timber. The longhouses must have been regarded as a statement of cultural identity – of symbolic importance to the settlers. They might have provided a sense of belonging to a community.

Evidence of economic change supports the idea of a Norse takeover in Orkney and Shetland. Fishing seems to have been a popular activity, but there was no large-scale exploitation. Economic changes are more likely to be brought about by large-scale colonization than by small numbers of the elite. In the case of fish consumption, unlike changes in language or costume, there would have been little incentive for the local population to adopt new practices except where this was necessary as a result of demographic change. The growth of fishing must therefore have been related to an increasing population.

Although the Norse cultural traditions have retained their importance in both the Northern and the Western Isles, it would be a mistake to see them as a purely Norse import uninfluenced by other cultures.

By the ninth century the Norse were leaving Ulster to colonize different lands in North America, across the great Atlantic Ocean. It is not certain whether the first of these left from Ulster or from Norway. Ulster Vikings heard of the great treasures that awaited them abroad, and we have seen that they reached as far as Istanbul in the far east of Europe. They left Ulster in their longships, not knowing what would befall them in the great West, but they must have come across the native Indian population on the east coast of what is now the United States. It is unlikely that they reached Central and South America, but the colonization of America must have been a very difficult business.

At Armagh the Christian Vikings welcomed the opportunity to bring the Church to the American barbarians. Armagh, of course, was a Norse city. The statue of Thor was present instead of statues of Christ and the Virgin Mary.

Eleventh- and twelfth-century written accounts mention some 190 farms in eastern parts and a further ninety in the west. There may have been as many as 4,000 living in Greenland at the peak of the colonization. The Norse settlement pattern is well documented. Fifty farms and twenty churches have been identified.

Cereal cultivation was impossible in lands like Greenland and Iceland, but domestic animals were reared. Much energy was expended in gathering winter fodder, and the animals were kept indoors for the winter. By April the farms would have been under much pressure. The Greenlanders became dependent on seals to eat, as is evident from the large number of bones found. Hounds may have been used for herding sheep, and as guard dogs. They may have formed a lord's hunting pack.

The Greenlanders traded in skins and ivory with Iceland and the North of Ireland to obtain grain, salt and iron.

It is of course uncertain whether or not the Vikings discovered America 500 years before Columbus. The archaeological evidence is sparse, and some of it has been invented. The discovery of America is mentioned in the Norse sagas. These were originally read as objective historical documents. Later they were dismissed as medieval fantasy. The modern view lies somewhere in between. The sagas probably retain an element of fact, but the story of the discovery of America is probably mythological.

The two primary accounts in *The Greenland Saga* and *Erik's Saga* were written in the Middle Ages. They appear to have been based on the same original material, but the stories diverge. After being blown off course on their way from Norway, the Vikings discovered new land south-west of Greenland. The land was thoroughly colonized and a large number of native barbarians lived there. The Vikings called it Vinland.

The site of Vinland has been much debated. Guesses range from Newfoundland to Labrador to Florida.

There was much incentive to sail from the coasts of Ulster and elsewhere in Ireland to explore foreign climes.

There were great halls and great rooms in the Viking settlements in Greenland. The sleeping apartments could hold up to about ninety people. The largest halls could also hold about the same number.

Only experienced Vikings could conquer far from the north coast of Ireland. Each longship could hold about thirty warriors as well as the large crew. In view of the distances involved it is surprising that the Vikings could conquer the warlike Red Indians.

The sagas appear to record much trading between the Indians and the Norsemen. Interesting archaeological finds point to some kind of intercourse between the two peoples.

The time at which the Greenland colony was disbanded is open to question. The Greenland colony was a significant Viking failure, and its disbandment marked the end of Norse expansion westwards, with the exception of Ulster.

In 1497 Newfoundland was rediscovered by John Cabot.

Ivar Bardarson, a cleric, arrived in Greenland in 1340 to administer the Church. Upon his return to Norway, he reported that by the mid-1350s nothing had been heard from the Western Settlement for many years. He mounted an expedition to investigate, but his longships only found deserted farms, the animals half wild, with no trace of people. The Western Settlement is therefore believed to have lasted until the mid-fourteenth century.

In 1406 a ship bound for Iceland from Norway was beset by storms and fog and driven to Greenland. The crew lived amongst the settlers for four years, and one of them got married. When they sailed for Norway in 1410 it was the last anyone heard of the colony.

Several reasons have been suggested for the failure of the colony. One suggestion is that climate change altered the route of the caribou, which the settlers depended on. Evidence is inconclusive, but most modern scholars believe the 'little ice age' could not have destroyed the Viking colonists because the great chill did not take place before 1600, by which time they had already disappeared. A decline in vegetation might have been caused by overgrazing by Norse livestock, but the settlers could always survive on fish. Another theory is that the Greenlanders, weakened by disease and malnutrition, were wiped out by the Black Death, but so far the skeletons that have been exhumed show no sign of the disease.

The colony was also affected by the decline in trade with Europe. By the fourteenth century, ivory had arrived from India, and furs from Russia were now available. This undermined the economic basis of the colony.

The late thirteenth- and early fourteenth-century *Historia Norvegiae* records conflict between the settlers and Inuit hunters, who used walrus teeth for missiles and sharpened stones for knives, but few historians now believe that the Inuit attacks were the sole reason for the colony's failure. The arrival of Inuits in the Western Settlement may well have been after it was already deserted. It is significant that Inuit artefacts are absent from the Norse sites. The Norse did not adopt Inuit skin-covered boats or kayaks or clothing styles; nor did they acquire harpoon-hunting technology.

Lack of adaptation seems to have been an important factor in the Norse decline. Norse farmers were tied to isolated pockets of pasture, capable of supporting domestic animals. They did not take much advantage of the sea. They clubbed seals when they reached land, whereas the Inuit hunted them by boat. Farmers lived in a regulated society controlled by powerful chiefs and Church officials. The social and economic structures of society rested upon payment of tithes to landowners, the Church and the Norwegian Crown.

The Church was an important influence. About twenty local churches were built, complete with stained glass, bells and vestments. Its main power centre was at Gardar, where a bishopric was established in a small stone cathedral dedicated to St Nicholas. The bishop's lands included a tithe barn, where the skulls of twenty-five walrus indicate the level of tithes. There was room for 150 cattle. Analysis of the bishop's skeleton revealed that he, unlike his parishioners, lived on a diet of land animals rather than seal meat.

Several sites provide archaeological evidence for the end of the Norse colony. At the bishop's palace at Gardar, nine skeletons of hunting dogs lay on the floors of stables and dwelling houses, buried beneath collapsed roof timbers of the mid-fourteenth century. The farm at GUS was abandoned around the same date. A single goat eventually returned, but, with no one left to care for him, he died from starvation.

When the roof started to collapse, a group of Inuit came and camped in the farmstead, now abandoned. They set the ruins alight, and they fled, leaving behind some of their belongings.

At Site W54 bio-archaeology has revealed the end of the farmstead, as warmth-loving insects in the lower farm levels were replaced by other insects. All that was left on the farms were cattle hoof marks and Arctic hares. In the hallway outside the larder were discovered the partial skeletons of the great hunting dogs. Cut marks in their bones revealed that these faithful hounds had provided the last supper of the occupants.

The tale of these starving inhabitants in the fourteenth century emphasizes the vast range of cultural behaviour to which the term 'Viking' has been applied.

A Time Chart of the Viking Age in Ireland, 795–900

The vast majority of the Viking raids are recorded in the Irish Annals – particularly the Annals of Ulster and the Annals of Clonmacnoise. As already mentioned, historians believe that Ireland (Ulster) was settled as early as the fourth century AD, but not many historians subscribe to this view; the later date of AD 795 seems to be more likely, chiefly because it is one of the traditions passed down by the Catholic Church.

795 Rathlin Island in North Antrim, Ulster, is attacked by the longships. The Vikings may also have sacked Lambay Island, near Dublin, burning it.

798 St Patrick's Island, also near Dublin, is burned. A cattle tribute is exacted and shrines are broken.

807 Inishmurray and Roscommon are raided and burned.

821 Wexford harbour may have been burned and plundered.

822 The island of Devenish and the town of Cork are sacked.

823 Bangor is raided and St Comgall's shrine is broken. Bishops and other learned men are slain.

825 Downpatrick is plundered. Movilla, with its timber churches, is burned.

827 Lusk is plundered and burned.

832 Armagh is plundered three times in one month, along with Muckno, Louth and Dunleek, with its churches. Tuathal mac Feradaig is carried off along with Adamnán's shrine. Maghera and Connor are plundered.

833 Clondalkin is plundered along with Lismore.

834 Glendalough, Slane and Connor are plundered.

835 Ferns and Clonmore, County Carlow, are plundered along with churches in West Munster. Druim Ing is sacked.

836 Kildare is plundered and half the church settlement is burned. There is great plunder and many captives are carried off or killed. Clonmore is ravaged on Christmas Eve; many are killed and many captives are carried off. The timber church at Glendalough is burned.

837 On Devenish, the churches, forts and dwellings are attacked. Clones is plundered.

839 Ferns and Cork in Leinster are burned, as are churches in the north of Ireland. Louth is plundered from Lough Neagh. Bishops, priests and other men of learning are carried off as captives and others are slain. Armagh, with its timber churches and its stone churches, is burned.

841 Clonenagh and Clonard are plundered. Killeigh is laid waste. Territories and churches are plundered from a base in County Louth.

842 Clonmacnoise is plundered, as well as Birr. Moran mac Inrachty, Abbot of Clogher, is captured by the Vikings and dies at their hands. Castledermot is plundered from Narrow Water, County Down. Kinnitty is plundered and Clonmacnoise is burned.

844 Clonfert is burned by the Norse from Lough Ree.

845 Forannan, Abbot of Armagh, is captured together with his insignia as he attempts to reach a ship on the Shannon estuary. A shrine of St Patrick is broken and carried off. Churches at Clonmacnoise, Clonfert, Terryglass and

Lorrha are burned and Nuadu mac Segeni is killed.

846 Baslick is plundered. Churches in County Kilkenny are plundered by a Norse expedition, but the raiders are eventually defeated.

847 Emly is plundered for the first time.

849 The King of Mugdorna is killed in clerical retirement.

850 The timber church at Trevet is burned with 260 Gaels inside. Vikings raid the Uí Neill from the River Shannon to the sea. Another church, with sixty people in it, is also burned.

852 Armagh is ravaged the Sunday after summer-Lent.

856 The timber church at Lusk is burned, and the Bishop of Slane is put to death.

860 Leighlin is plundered and many captives are taken and killed.

864 The joint King of Mide is drowned at Clonard by the Norse.

866 Clonfert is plundered by Tomrar the Jarl, who is killed through the agency of St Brendan three days after reaching his base.

867 Treachery takes place in Lismore and Abbot Martan dies.

869 Armagh is again plundered by Amlaíb and burned with its timber chapels. One thousand are either killed or carried off with great plunder. Eodis Donngaiule is killed in Castledermot. Kilmore in County Armagh is again sacked.

879 Mael mac Drunnmail, head of Armagh, and Mochta, a master of learning, are captured.

881 The timber churches at Cianban are destroyed and many people are carried off. Barith, a wealthy man, is killed.

882 Armagh is raided by Flann Sinna and the Norse.

883 Lismore is burned by the son of Ivar.

886 Kildare is plundered and many captives are taken, including the vice-abbot.

888 The abbot and vice-abbot of Cloyne are slain.

890 Glendalough is raided again, along with Dunlane, Donaghpatrick and Ardbraccan.

891 Kildare and Clonard are plundered.

895 Armagh is plundered and captives are taken.

898 Armagh is plundered from Lough Foyle.

900 Kildare is again plundered and a relic of St Patrick is carried off by the Norse.

Conclusions

There was nothing the Church of Rome could do to alleviate the position. Viking raids were common throughout Europe as the Norsemen spread their net of conquest. It was little consolation that the Norse at length became farmers and, in some respects, peaceful people. The Irish contained the Norse menace at the Battle of Clontarf.

In Europe, the Vikings of Normandy eventually evolved into the Normans, who launched an attack on Ireland in 1177.

The Vikings that took to Christianity were perhaps just as Christian as the Gaels, whom they at first conquered.

At Armagh the Church tradition lingered on, despite the Norse ravages; the Christians forgave the Vikings for their incursions even though they killed many priests and abbots.

The Vikings were perhaps not as hated as the Normans or the English, even though the Viking ascendancy lasted from the eighth century through to 1014 – a period of about 300 years. The Gaels put up some resistance to the raiders, as witness the round towers and the fortification of monasteries and convents.

The Pope could only put his blessing upon Irish efforts, though he was to some extent not taken by the hostile Norman monarchy in England and France. This was the age of the Angevins.

The ordinary Gael and some of the clergy made pilgrimages to Rome and the holy places of Europe, risking their lives abroad as well as in Ireland. The Irish had been regarded as the harbingers of civilization and had preached at the court of Emperor Charlemagne.

Today the Vikings have been consigned to the history books, the memory of their cruelty almost forgotten.

The Normans' ascendancy in Ireland did not end until the War of the Roses in the fifteenth century.

Many books have been published on the history of the Norse, and most agree that the Vikings were a harsh-tempered people, despite their eventual conversion to Christianity.

Today Norway, Sweden and Denmark are small powers governed by monarchies. By the eighth century they had established some sort of unity, and the result of that unity was the Viking raiders. It took several days for the Norsemen to sail from the north of Europe to the warmer climate of the Pretannic (or British) Isles.

At first the Vikings were pagan, and the Pope in Rome regarded them at first as not open to reason or to conversion. He spurred Europe on with the hope of freeing Ireland from the pagans. He also wanted to oust them from England, which was at that time a small power made up of different kingdoms.

The modern Irishman does not hate the Vikings. They are part of Ireland's historic heritage. The Normans and the English, on the other hand, sought to suppress the island, often from a northern base, for Dublin is geographically in the north of Ireland. Though Armagh, which lives on as the focus of the Church in Ireland, was sacked and burned so many times by the Norsemen, Ulster stood firm.

It could well have been a monk at the top of a round tower in Antrim who saw the first longships approaching the mainland after sacking and burning the monastery on Rathlin Island in 795.

Select Bibliography

Colmán Etchingham: *Viking Raids on Irish Church Settlements in the Ninth Century* (Maynooth Monographs, 1996).

Else Roesdahl: *The Vikings* (Penguin, 1987).

Eric Christiansen: *The Norsemen in the Viking Age* (Wiley-Blackwell, 2002).

Hector McDonnell: *Irish Round Towers* (Wooden Books, 2005).

Jacqueline Simpson: *Everyday Life in the Viking Age* (B. T. Batsford, 1967).

John Haywood: *The Penguin Historical Atlas of the Vikings* (Penguin, 1995).

Judith Jesch: *Women in the Viking Age* (The Boydell Press, 1991).

Julian Richards: *Vikings* (Oxford, 2005).

Martin Arnold: *The Vikings* (The History Press, 2008).

Morgan Llywelyn: *Brian Boru* (The O'Brien Press, 1990).

Morgan Llywelyn: *The Vikings in Ireland* (The O'Brien Press, 1996).

Peter Sawyer (editor): *The Oxford Illustrated History of the Vikings* (Oxford, 1997).

Rudolf Poertner: *The Vikings: Rise and Fall of the North Sea Kings* (St James Press, 1975).